RUMAN
ENGLISH PICTURE DICTIONARY

By Majeda Hourani
Illustrated by Abdullah Qawariq
Designed by Asem Naser

RUMAN
ENGLISH PICTURE DICTIONARY

Copyright © RumanLLC 2019 All rights reserved
Without limiting the rights under copyright reserved above, no part of this publication may be reproduced, stored in or introduced into a retrieval system, or transmitted, in any form, or by any means (electronic, mechanical, photocopying, recording, or otherwise), without the prior written permission of both the copyright owner

ISBN 978-1-7340924-9-3

جميع الحقوق محفوظة لشركة رمان
لا يجوز طباعة أو ترجمة أو نقل أي أجزاء منه بأي شكل من الأشكال إلا بإذن خطي مسبق من الناشر
الطبعة الأولى نوفمبر 2020

Publisher: Ruman LLC
E-mail: rumanllc@gmail.com
Website: www.ruman-llc.com

About the Ruman English Picture Dictionary

Teaching vocabulary in context has been proven to be an incredibly effective method to reinforce memorization. Therefore, Ruman introduces its first English Picture Dictionary following this method.

The Ruman English Picture Dictionary is a foldout collection of twenty delightful posters targeting different subjects related to our daily lives. Each poster is surrounded by up to thirty-five nouns and five to ten verbs each represented by a unique drawing. This feature allows for the visualization of all vocabulary words without the necessity of including any translation.

This colorful and highly visual dictionary introduces beginners to more than 1550 key vocabulary words in the English language. The posters focus on scenes that are familiar to children, such as home life, the classroom, city life, basic shapes, antonyms, and animals. Learners will be drawn to revisit these detailed depictions of the scenes, each time improving their memory. In addition, this dictionary has main characters that will be followed throughout the posters allowing learners to connect to them.

This dictionary is also highly socially engaged as it purposefully conveys positive messages related to children's rights, ethnic diversity, inclusion of children with disabilities, animal welfare, and gender equality. Ruman believes that these messages of inclusion and diversity reflect the foundations of the culture and society that we want to teach to our children.

The Ruman English Picture Dictionary is intended mainly as a classroom resource to help primary age students consolidate and enlarge their vocabulary. However, it can be also used as a personal learning resource at home. Each dictionary can be accompanied by a set of learning cards developed in order to keep this resource exciting and engaging for the children.

The Dictionary contents

Family Tree 6

Classroom 8

School 10

Daily verbs 12

Fruits and vegetables 14

Food and Drink 16

Body and appearance 18

Emotions and feelings 20

Clothes 22

House 24

Kitchen and garden 26

Hobbies — 28

Professions and Jobs — 30

Weather and seasons — 32

Transportation and Travel — 34

City — 36

Farm — 38

Animals — 40

Antonyms — 42

Numbers — 44

Time — 46

Colors and shapes — 48

Family Tree

Classroom

 wall clock
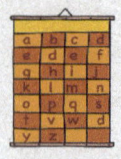 numbers
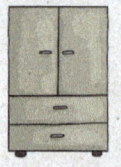 alphabet
 cupboard

 student
 ruler
 papers
 shelf
 desk
 pen
 pencil
 days of the week

 backpack
 table
 glue
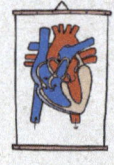 picture
 notebook

8

 bookcase
 sharpener
 eraser
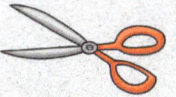 scissors
 pencil case
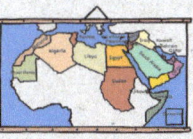 map

 teacher 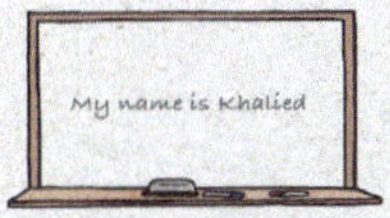
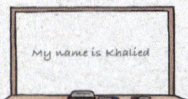 whiteboard
 book
 colors
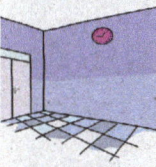 wall
 computer
 toys

 story
 binder 
 desk
 chair
 wastebasket
 window

School

language class

history and geography class

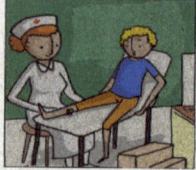
nurse's office/room

physical education

math class

science class

library

theater

music class

art class

computer lab

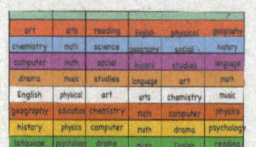
program/schedule

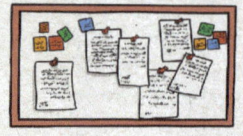
bulletin board

crosswalk

 cipal's office

 cafeteria

 students lockers

 science lab

 parking lot

 parents/Family

 cooker

 nurse

 principal

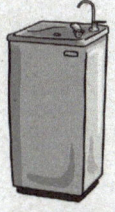 drinking water fountain

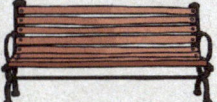 bench

 School bus

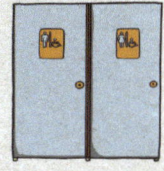 playground

bathrooms

Daily Verbs

Fruits and Vegetables

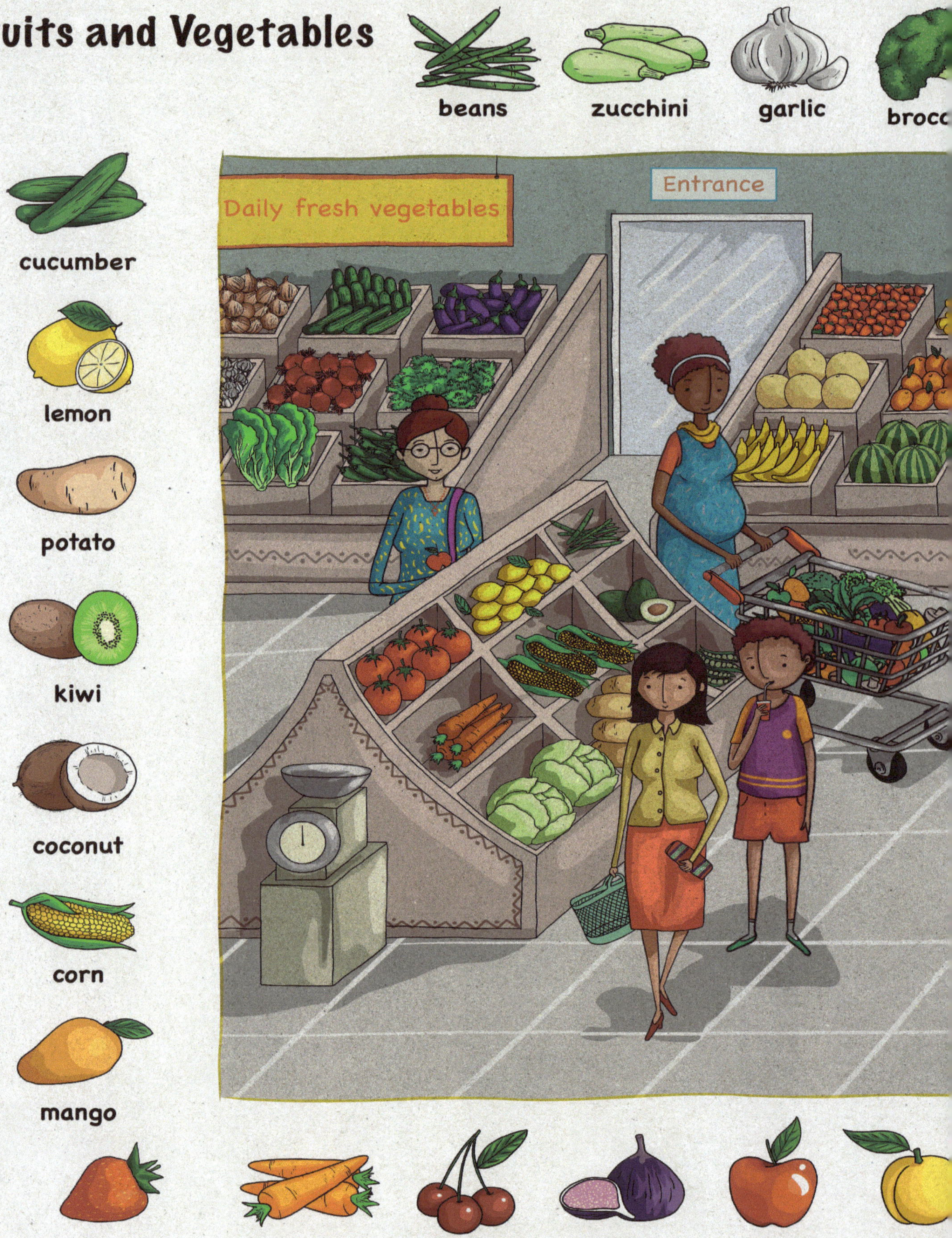

 beans

 zucchini

 garlic

 brocc

 cucumber

 lemon

 potato

 kiwi

 coconut

 corn

 mango

 strawberry

 carrots

 cherry

 fig

 apple

 apric

pepper   radish   cabbage   peas   celery   lettuce   parsley

beet

eggplant

tomato

onions

orange

pomegranate

melon

grape   peach   pineapple   avocado   watermelon   banana

Food and Drink

 chicken
 oil
 olive oil
 honey
 soft drink

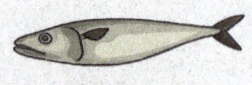 fish
 meat
 sausage
 bread
 pita bread
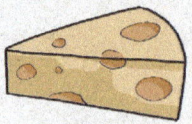 cheese
 butter
 pastries

 pizza
 biscuit
 chocolate
 chickpea
 eggs
 milk

 spices
 fava beans
 tomato sauce
 jam
 canned food
 water
 juice  
 salt
 lollipop
 cake
 tea
 coffee
 lentil
 rice
 sour yogurt
 chips
 sugar
 pasta
 mixed nuts

17

Body and Appearance

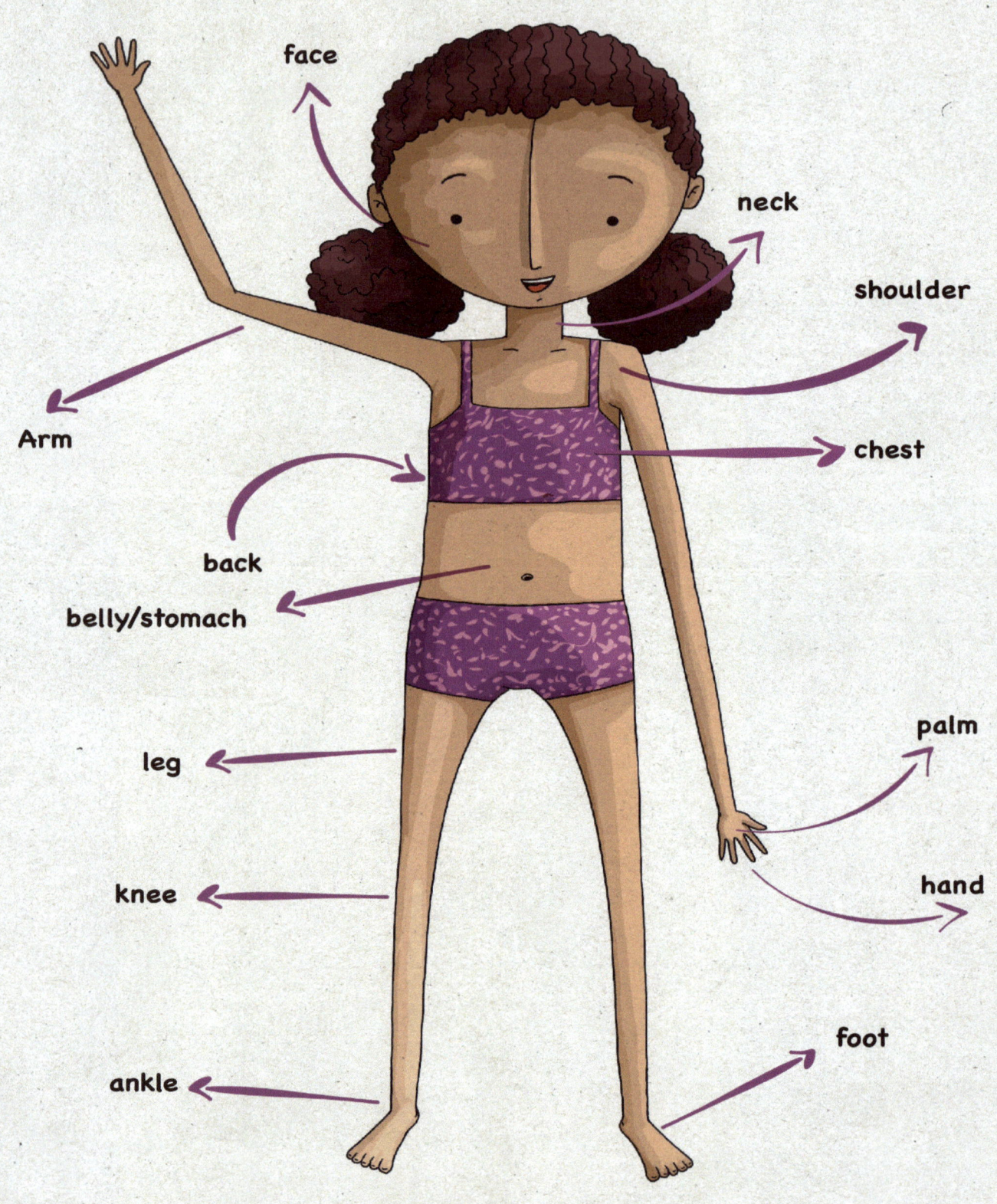

Feelings

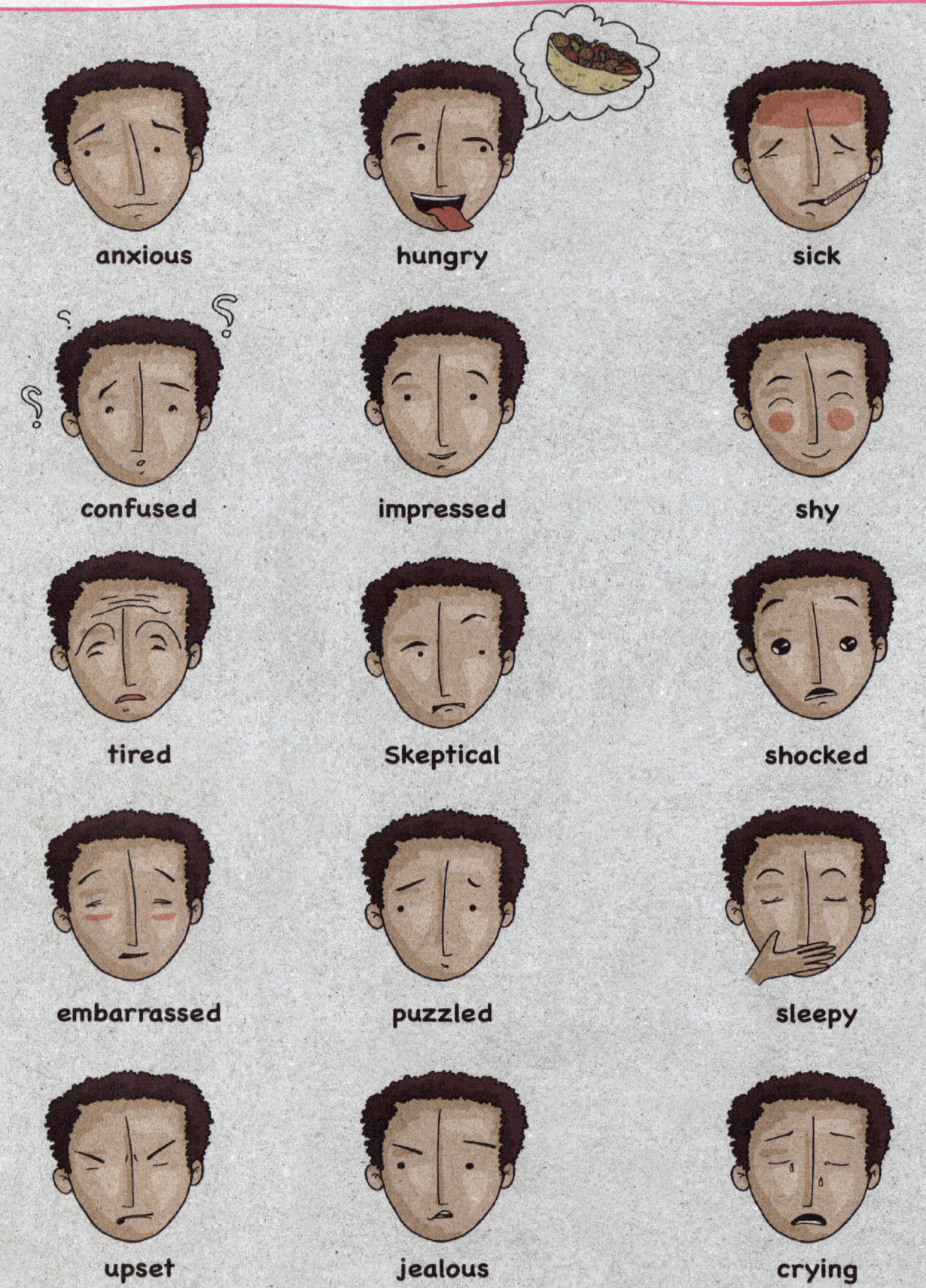

 scared

 sad

 happy

 angry

 cold

 surprised

 proud

 frustrated

 bored

 relaxed

 depressed

 excited

laughing

 longing

 nervous

Clothes

 sport shoes
 boots
 high heels shoes
flip flops
shoes
 sandals

 swimsuit

 sweater

 shirt

 t-shirt

 jacket

 skirt

Women's Clothing

Sports Clothing

 tie
 robe
 coat
 pajamas
 jeans
 shorts

22

 slippers
 gloves
 belt
 perfume
 watch
 sunglasses
 hat

 undershirt
 underpants
 dress
 blouse
 cloak
 scarf

Men's Clothing

Children's Clothing

 suit
 handbag
 earrings
 ring
 necklace
 wallet
 socks

House

curtain

couch

throw pillow

pillow

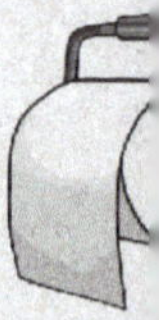

toilet paper

door

closet

carpet

balcony

window

office

bedroom

garage

bathroom

sink

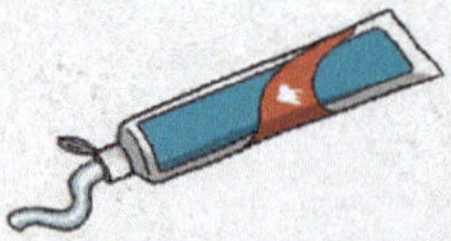

toothpaste

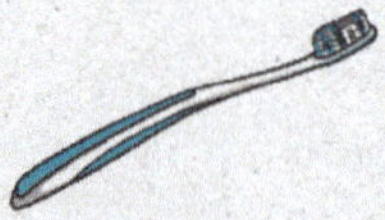

toothbrush

towel

stairs

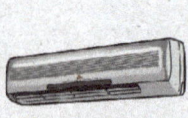
air conditioner

tap

24

 painting

 lamp

 fan

 shower sponge

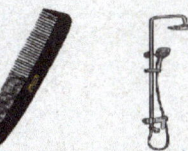 comb

 shower

 key hanger

 clothes hanger

 coffee table

 television

 duvet

 photo frame

 toilet

 soap

 studio

 bedroom

 living room

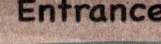 Entrance

 scale

 laundry basket

 bed

 mirror

shampoo

 tub

Kitchen and Garden

 tree
 fence
 water hose
 dishwashing soap

 grass
 flower Basin
 fountain
 watering can
 can opener
 pot
 vacuum cleaner

 broom
 teapot 
 kettle
 cup
 dish
 pot-holder
 bowl
colander

Hobbies

Professions and Jobs

Seasons and Weather

tree leaves

butterflies

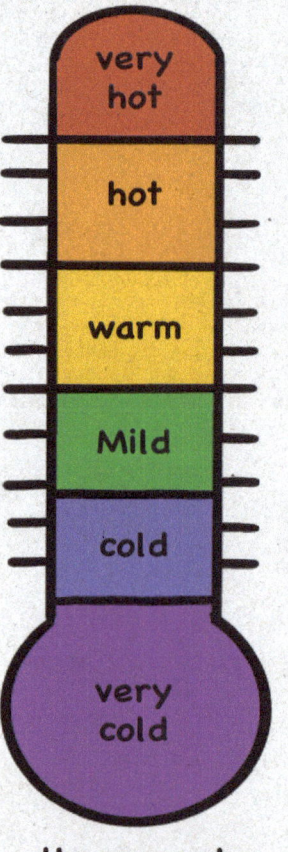
thermometer

flowers

fog

wind/windy

cloudy partly cloudy cloud sun-sunny

storm/stormy

lightning

rain/rainy

snow/snowy

fireplace umbrella spring rain

33

Transportation and Travel

Air Balloon

highway

street

traveller

bus stop

airplane

helicopter

train

railway

taxi

car

truck

sidewalk

crosswalk   bicycle

motorcycle

ticket

passport

Submarine

boat

steamship

sailing ship

ambulance

bus

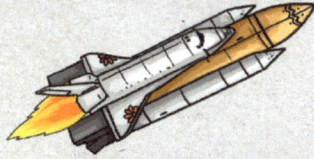
rocket

35

City

Farm

hay

stable

tractor

scarecrow

cow

bull

camel

horse

donkey

sheep

goat

cat

chicken

 seeds

 butterfly

 pigeon

 bird

 peacock

 ant

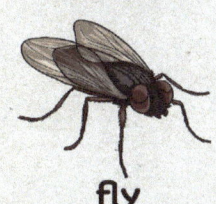 bee

 fly

 spider

 chick

 rabbit

 rooster

 duck

 dog

 hedgehog

 mouse

Animals

shark

fish

zebra

whale

ostrich

elephant

deer

giraffe

owl

parrot

hawk

hoopoe

Antonyms

Numbers

⭐ Numbers from 0 to 10:

0 zero	1 one
2 two 	3 three 	4 four
5 five 	6 six 	7 seven 
8 eight	9 nine	10 ten

⭐ Ordinal numbers:

first   second   third   fourth   fifth   sixth   seventh   eighth   ninth   tenth

Numbers from 11 to 100:

11 eleven	12 twelve	13 thirteen	14 fourteen	15 fifteen	16 sixteen	17 seventeen	18 eighteen	19 ninteen	20 twenty
21 twenty one	22 twenty two	23 twenty three	24 twenty four	25 twenty five	26 twenty six	27 twenty seven	28 twenty eight	29 twenty nine	30 thirty
31 thirty one	32 thirty two	33 thirty three	34 thirty four	35 thirty five	36 thirty six	37 thirty seven	38 thirty eight	39 thirty nine	40 forty
41 forty one	42 forty two	43 forty three	44 forty four	45 forty five	46 forty six	47 forty seven	48 forty eight	49 forty nine	50 fifty
51 fifty one	52 fifty two	53 fifty three	54 fifty four	55 fifty five	56 fifty six	57 fifty seven	58 fifty eight	59 fifty nine	60 sixty
61 sixty one	62 sixty two	63 sixty three	64 sixty four	65 sixty five	66 sixty six	67 sixty seven	68 sixty eight	69 sixty nine	70 seventy
71 seventy one	72 seventy two	73 seventy three	74 seventy four	75 seventy five	76 seventy six	77 seventy seven	78 seventy eight	79 seventy nine	80 eighty
81 eighty one	82 eighty two	83 eighty three	84 eighty four	85 eighty five	86 eighty six	87 eighty seven	88 eighty eight	89 eighty nine	90 ninety
91 ninety one	92 ninety two	93 ninety three	94 ninety four	95 ninety five	96 ninety six	97 ninety seven	98 ninety eight	99 ninety nine	100 one hundred

thousand	→	1000
million	→	1,000,000
billion	→	1,000,000,000
Trillion	→	1,000,000,000,000

Time

⭐ **Times of the day**

| night | early morning | morning | noon | dusk | evening | night |

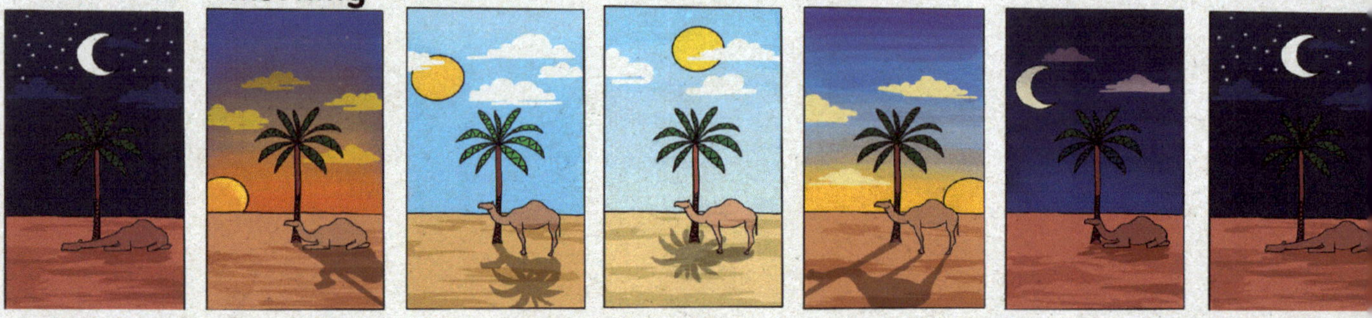

⭐ **Units of the time**

| day | hour | minute | second |
| 24:00:00 | 01:00:00 | 00:01:00 | 00:00:01 |

week

Sunday | Monday | Tuesday | Wednesday | Thursday | Friday | Saturday

year

2019

month

46

⭐ **What time is it?**

One O'clock	 Two O'clock	 Three O'clock	 Four O'clock
 Five O'clock	 Six O'clock	 Seven O'clock	 Eight O'clock
 Nine O'clock	 Ten O'clock	 Eleven O'clock	 Twelve O'clock

⭐ **Reading the time**

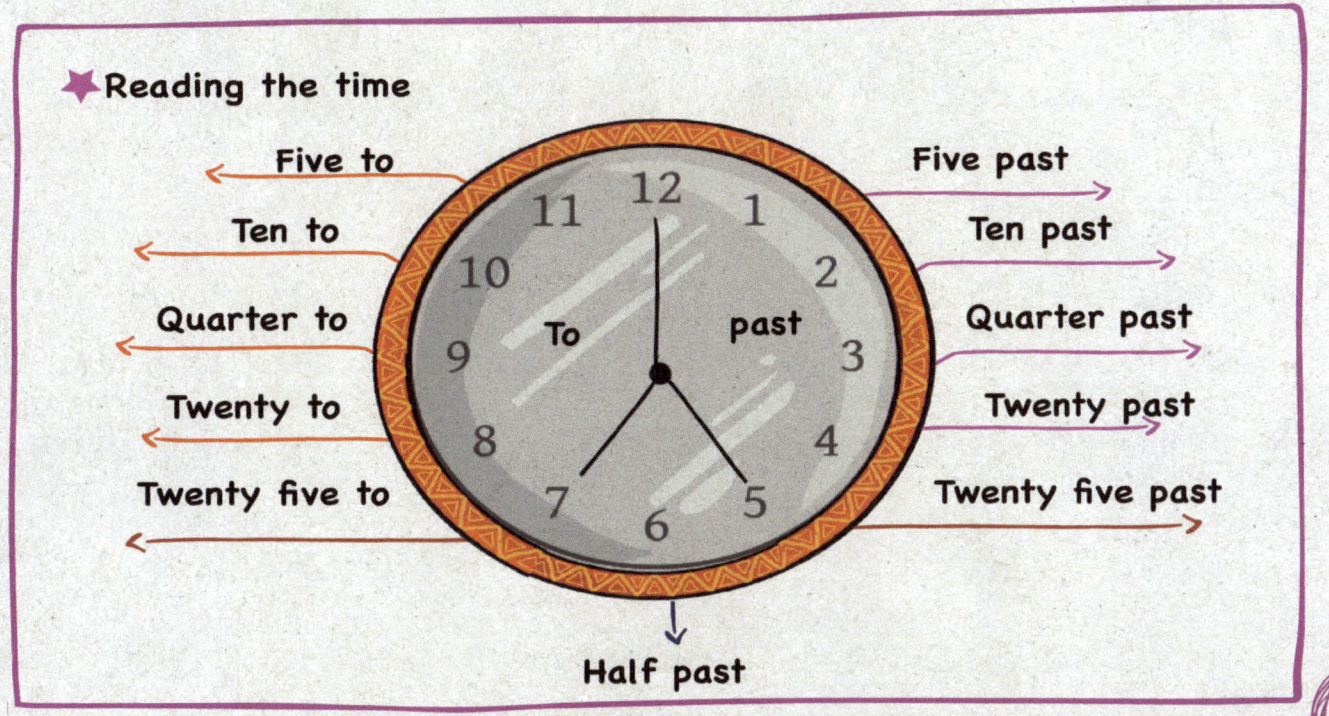

Five to — Five past
Ten to — Ten past
Quarter to — Quarter past
Twenty to — Twenty past
Twenty five to — Twenty five past
Half past

47

Colors and Shapes

spiral line   vertical line   horizontal line   wavy line   curve line

apricot

beige

golden

yellow

lime

olive

green

turquoise

blue

purple   pink   red   maroon Scarlet   orange   brown   grey   white   black

48